My Daddy Makes the Best Motorcycle in the Whole Wide World —
The Harley-Davidson

by Jean Davidson

Illustrations by Theresa Hammerquist

The Guest Cottage
WOODRUFF, WISCONSIN

My name is Jeannie.
I am eight years old.

For all the children in the world who love motorcycles —
Follow your dreams!

To my mother and father who gave me all the joys of childhood.
—J. D.

My last name is D A V I D S O N.
My daddy is Gordon Davidson.
He works at a big factory where
they make motorcycles.

I love to ride on motorcycles.
My daddy takes me for rides all the time.
I ride in the sidecar and we go FAST!

Sometimes we hit a bump.
My daddy and I laugh and laugh.
"Let's go FASTER, Daddy!"

My mommy and my sister like to ride.
When we all go, I get the best seat.
I ride right behind my daddy.

I hang on tight.
It makes me feel *special*.

My daddy learned to ride
motorcycles from his father.

And that's *my* grandfather.

My grandfather had two brothers and a best friend, Bill Harley.
Going fishing was their favorite thing to do.
It was a long way to their favorite fishing spot.

Sometimes they rode
their bicycles.
It was hard work going
up all the hills.
One day they thought,
"Why not put a motor
on a bicycle?

We wouldn't have to
pedal so hard.
We could have FUN
on the way."

And that's why they started making these motorcycles
that I have been talking about.

Their mommy said, "No More Mess in My House!"

So their daddy built them their very own shed in the backyard. Now they could be as messy as they wanted. They all worked together and made their first motorcycles.

Janet, their big sister, painted their names on each gas tank.

Henry, their friend from school, bought the first one. He rode up and down the streets in his neighborhood. He liked to show off on his new motorcycle.

Pretty soon people from all over wanted a motorcycle.

The mailman wanted one to deliver the mail.

The fireman wanted one
to get to the fire fast.

The policeman wanted
one to chase the robbers.

The army wanted one for their soldiers to use in far away countries.

And . . .

Now their shed got too small and messy.
Everyone helped and they built a factory.

Every year their factory got bigger and bigger.

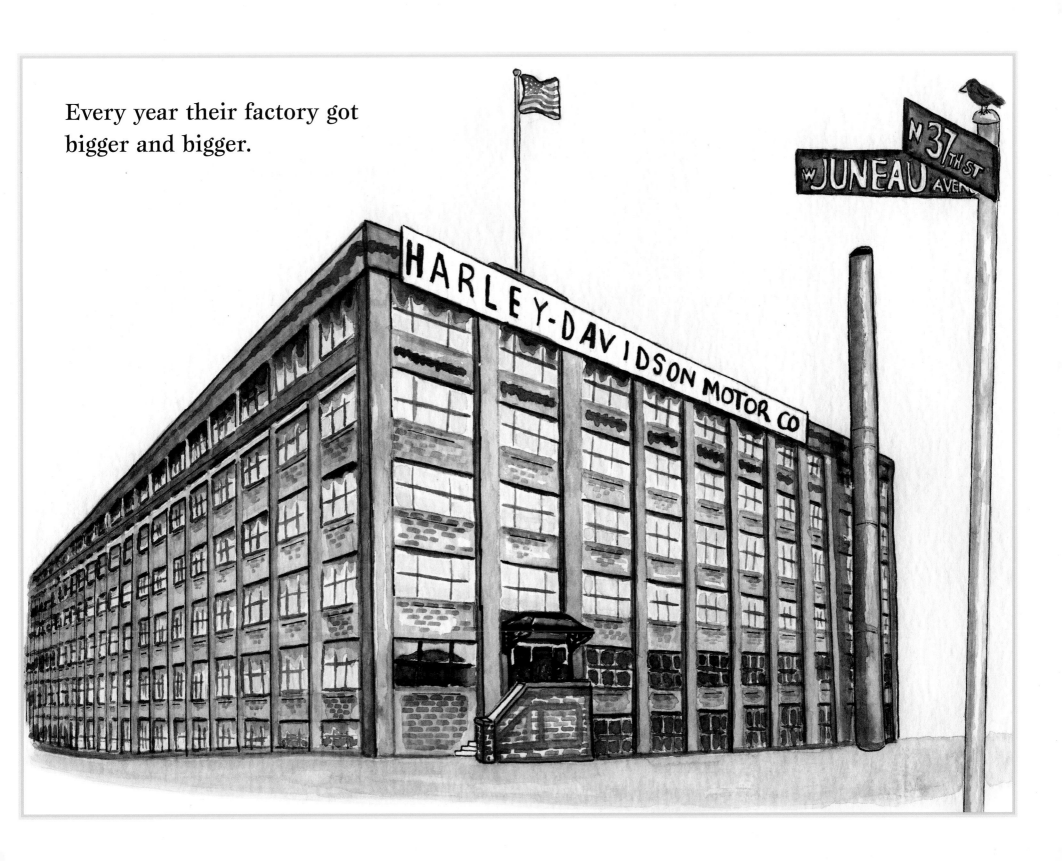

I go to the factory with my daddy a lot.
It is noisy.

Lots of people work there making
motorcycles.

ASSEMBLY LINE

They all know me.
Sometimes they let me ride the assembly line.
Round and round I go.

I go to school.
I am in second grade.
School is FUN!

My daddy picks me up from school
with his motorcycle.
All my friends want to go for a ride.

Every summer, my daddy and
I go to the motorcycle races.
There is a BIG racetrack near
my house.
We live in Milwaukee.
It is in the state
of Wisconsin.

Motorcycle races are LOUD!
The racers go fast and bump into each other.
The winner gets to the finish line first.
I yell and clap for my favorites.

I am only eight years old NOW.
But when I grow up, I want my very own motorcycle.

NORM ZIERK

JEAN DAVIDSON is an internationally known author and speaker. She is the granddaughter of Walter Davidson, one of the founders and first president of Harley-Davidson Motor Company. Her father, Gordon Davidson, was the vice president of manufacturing. Her first two books, *Growing Up Harley-Davidson* and *Jean Davidson's Harley-Davidson Family Album* are now found around the world. She travels extensively speaking about the personal stories of the Harley-Davidson legacy.

Motorcycle riders tell her over and over how, like her, their love of motorcycles started at an early age.

My Daddy Makes the Best Motorcycle in the Whole Wide World — the Harley-Davidson is her first children's book. Being a lifelong teacher and Davidson family member, she wants to bring the Harley-Davidson stories to children around the world.

She lives in Milwaukee, Wisconsin and can be reached at: www.jeandavidson.com or email jean@jeandavidson.com

NORM ZIERK

THERESA HAMMERQUIST developed her painting talent as a direct result of the Prayer of Jabez. She presently lives in the Midwest with her husband and their three children.

She can be reached at tevahammerquist@aol.com

Dedicated to my young apprentices,
my Barnabus', and to my best friend,
for the beautiful gift of painting.
— T. H.

ISBN 1-930596-26-X
Published by the Guest Cottage, Inc.
PO Box 848
Woodruff, WI 54568
800/333-8122
www.theguestcottage.com
Please write or call to request a free catalog of other publications by the Guest Cottage.

Book design and production: Pat Linder/Linder Creative Services
Scanning: Ken B. Webb, Digital Artist

Library of Congress Cataloging-in-Publication Data

Davidson, Jean, 1937-
  My daddy makes the best motorcycles in the whole wide world, the Harley-Davidson / by Jean Davidson ; illustrated by Theresa Hammerquist.
    p. cm.
  ISBN 1-930596-26-X (hardcover)
  1. Harley Davidson motorcycle—Juvenile literature. 2. Davidson family—Juvenile literature. 3. Davidson, Jean, 1937—-Childhood and youth—Juvenile literature. 4. Harley-Davidson Incorporated—History—Juvenile literature. I. Hammerquist, Theresa, ill. II. Title.
  TL448.H3D36 2004
  629.227'5'0973—dc22
                                    2004003876

Printed in Canada